WWW.APEXEDITIONS.COM

Copyright © 2025 by Apex Editions, Mendota Heights, MN 55120. All rights reserved. No part of this book may be reproduced or utilized in any form or by any means without written permission from the publisher.

Apex is distributed by North Star Editions:
sales@northstareditions.com | 888-417-0195

Produced for Apex by Red Line Editorial.

Photographs ©: iStockphoto, cover, 1, 18–19, 44–45; EMPPL PA Wire/AP Images, 4–5; Shutterstock Images, 6–7, 8–9, 10–11, 12–13, 14–15, 16–17, 20–21, 22–23, 24–25, 27, 36–37, 38–39, 42–43, 46–47, 50–51, 52–53, 54–55, 56–57; AP Images, 28–29; Paul Harris/Archive Photos/Getty Images, 30–31; Phelan M. Ebenhack/AP Images, 32–33; Frank Duenzl/picture-alliance/dpa/AP Images, 34–35; Stefan Jacobs/Alamy, 40–41; Mark Sears/NOAA, 49; Red Line Editorial, 58–59

Library of Congress Control Number: 2023922995

ISBN
979-8-89250-211-5 (hardcover)
979-8-89250-232-0 (paperback)
979-8-89250-273-3 (ebook pdf)
979-8-89250-253-5 (hosted ebook)

Printed in the United States of America
Mankato, MN
082024

NOTE TO PARENTS AND EDUCATORS

Apex books are designed to build literacy skills in striving readers. Exciting, high-interest content attracts and holds readers' attention. The text is carefully leveled to allow students to achieve success quickly.

TABLE OF CONTENTS

Chapter 1
ORCA SURPRISE 4
Chapter 2
ORCAS AND HUMANS 8
Chapter 3
FIGHTING FOR FISH 16
That's Wild!
FISHING TOGETHER 26
Chapter 4
ORCA ATTACKS IN CAPTIVITY 28
Chapter 5
ORCAS AND BOATS 38
That's Wild!
HUMANS HELP OUT 48
Chapter 6
LIVING TOGETHER 51

MAP • 58
COMPREHENSION QUESTIONS • 60
GLOSSARY • 62
TO LEARN MORE • 63
ABOUT THE AUTHOR • 63
INDEX • 64

Chapter 1

ORCA SURPRISE

It is January 1911. An Antarctic explorer stands on his ship. The ship's dogs and a photographer wait on the ice below. Then, the explorer spots a group of orcas. The orcas swim toward the dogs and photographer. Then they disappear underwater.

> Captain Robert Scott led two trips to Antarctica. His group was the second to reach the South Pole.

Sometimes, orcas spy-hop. They stick their heads out of the water to look around.

Suddenly, the ice shatters. The orcas smash it from below. Cracks and booms fill the air. The orcas rise to the surface. Their sharp teeth are ready. But the orcas do not attack. They pause. Then they swim away. Everyone is safe.

LOOKING FOR SEALS

Orcas in the Antarctic find prey on the ice. They often attack seals. Orcas may break the ice. That knocks seals into the water. Other times, orcas make waves. The moving water sweeps seals off the ice.

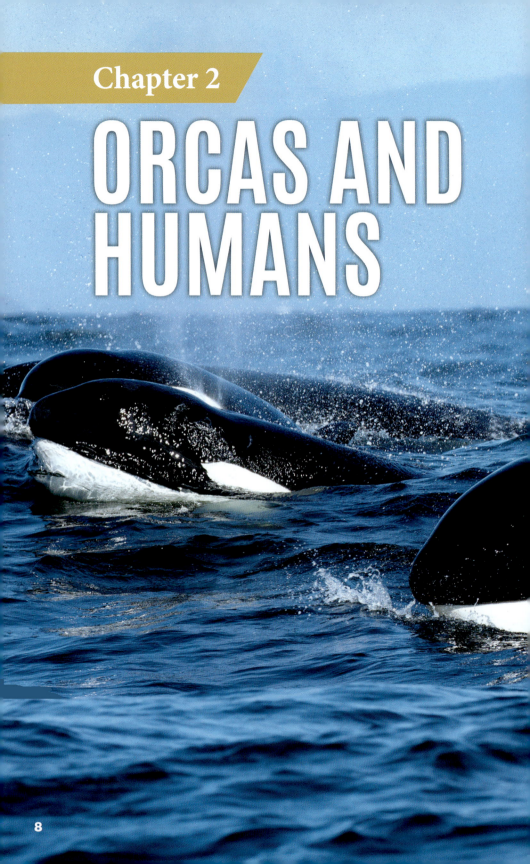

Chapter 2
ORCAS AND HUMANS

Orcas are ocean mammals. Orcas travel in family groups called pods. Some pods have just a few orcas. Other pods have 30 orcas or more. All orca pods are matrilineal. This means the female orcas are in charge. Females take care of the young. They also teach hunting and communication.

Orcas are a type of dolphin.

Orcas are also called killer whales. That's because they are deadly hunters. Orcas are carnivores. Their prey differs depending on where orcas live. Many types of orcas eat fish. Other types eat sea mammals such as dolphins and walruses. Some orcas even hunt other whales.

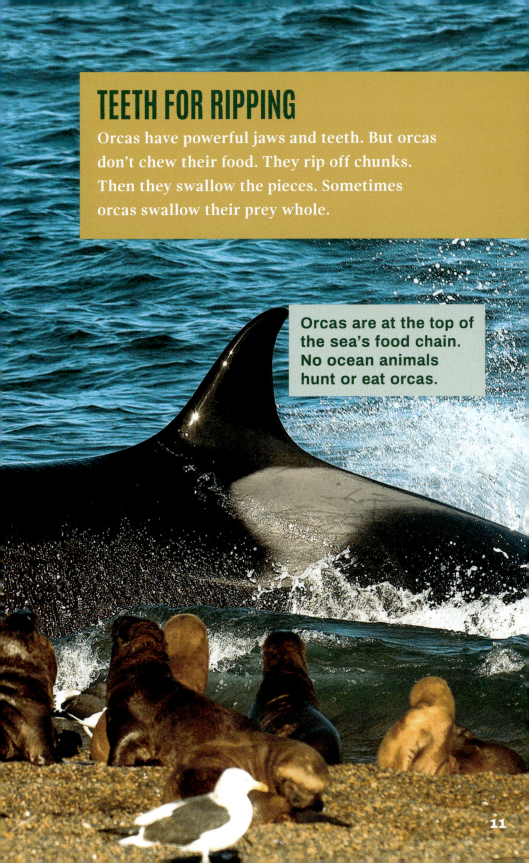

TEETH FOR RIPPING

Orcas have powerful jaws and teeth. But orcas don't chew their food. They rip off chunks. Then they swallow the pieces. Sometimes orcas swallow their prey whole.

Orcas are at the top of the sea's food chain. No ocean animals hunt or eat orcas.

Mother orcas teach their babies how to communicate. That helps them hunt.

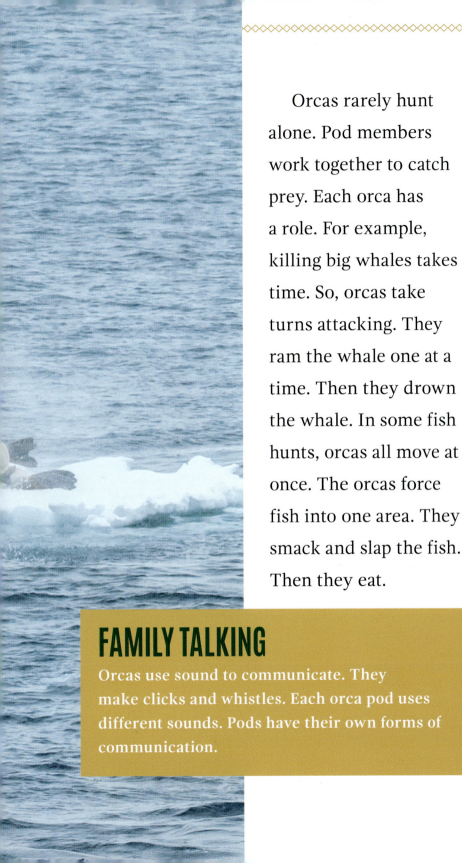

Orcas rarely hunt alone. Pod members work together to catch prey. Each orca has a role. For example, killing big whales takes time. So, orcas take turns attacking. They ram the whale one at a time. Then they drown the whale. In some fish hunts, orcas all move at once. The orcas force fish into one area. They smack and slap the fish. Then they eat.

FAMILY TALKING

Orcas use sound to communicate. They make clicks and whistles. Each orca pod uses different sounds. Pods have their own forms of communication.

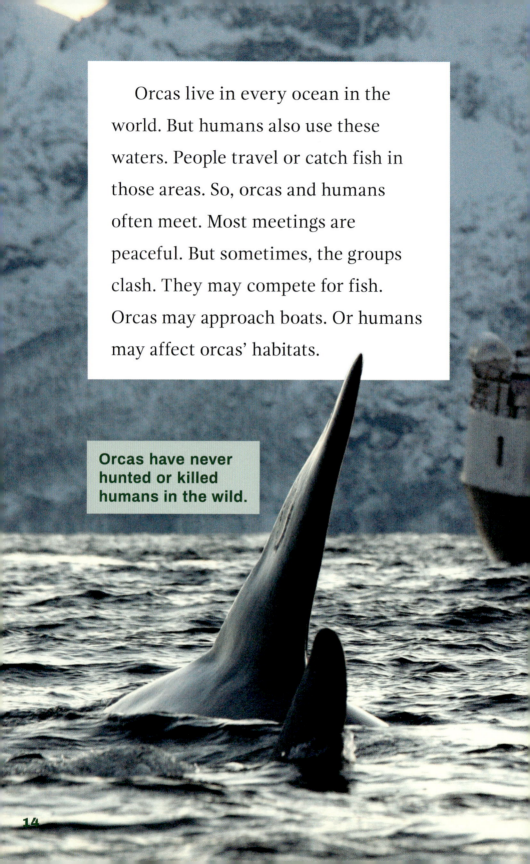

Orcas live in every ocean in the world. But humans also use these waters. People travel or catch fish in those areas. So, orcas and humans often meet. Most meetings are peaceful. But sometimes, the groups clash. They may compete for fish. Orcas may approach boats. Or humans may affect orcas' habitats.

Orcas have never hunted or killed humans in the wild.

HOW BIG?

Some orcas weigh up to 20,000 pounds (9,000 kg). That's as heavy as two elephants. The huge size can scare humans. They think orcas may hurt them. But orcas rarely attack humans.

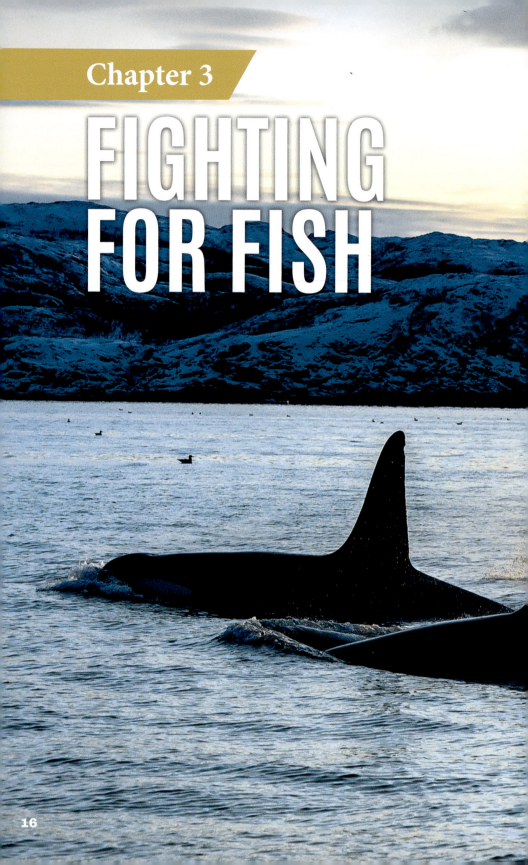

Chapter 3
FIGHTING FOR FISH

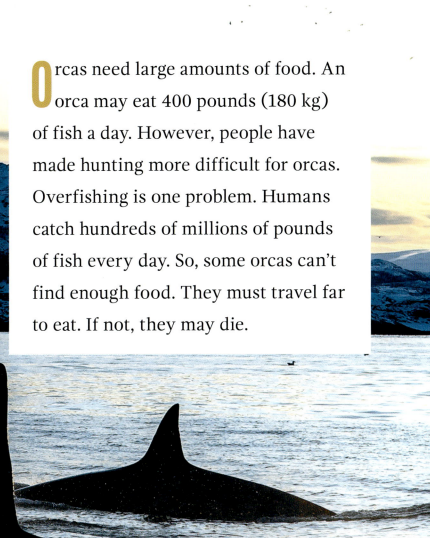

Orcas need large amounts of food. An orca may eat 400 pounds (180 kg) of fish a day. However, people have made hunting more difficult for orcas. Overfishing is one problem. Humans catch hundreds of millions of pounds of fish every day. So, some orcas can't find enough food. They must travel far to eat. If not, they may die.

Orcas can travel about 100 miles (160 km) a day.

Southern Resident orcas eat Chinook salmon. These fish are the biggest salmon in the world.

HUMAN HARM

In 2005, Southern Resident orcas became endangered. Humans killing orcas is part of the problem. Overfishing and pollution are harmful, too.

Southern Resident orcas live in the North Pacific. These orcas hunt mostly salmon. Humans also catch salmon in that area. In the past, many fishers there disliked orcas. They worried orcas would eat all the salmon. So, the fishers brought guns on their boats. They shot and killed some orcas.

Some orcas swim through the Indian Ocean. In the past, these orcas ate mostly seals and penguins. In the 1990s, their diet began to change. Fishers in the area used longlines to catch toothfish. These lines hooked many fish at once. A few orcas began stealing fish from the lines. Those orcas taught the trick to others. Soon, whole pods were stealing fish. The orcas had changed their hunting habits and diets.

FINDING FOOD

Orcas find prey with echolocation. Their sound waves hit prey and bounce back to them. However, fishing boats may block the sound waves. Human noise gets in the way, too. That makes it harder for orcas to hunt.

Some fishers used fishing pots instead of lines. Orcas can't get into the pots.

Orcas have the second largest brains of any animal.

Orcas are smart animals. They have good memories and learn skills quickly. So, orcas often return to the same fishing boats. They steal fish over and over again. Fishers try to avoid this problem. Some fishers travel to new areas. But this action can be costly. And it doesn't always work.

HARD TO SPOT

Orcas' colors help them stay hidden. Their underbellies are white. From below, they blend in with the sun's light on the water. And their black tops match the dark sea. People looking down from boats might not see orcas.

Bottom trawl nets catch fish along the ocean floor.

When orcas steal fish, fishers can't sell as much. They lose money. Orcas might also break fishing tools. But stealing fish can also harm the orcas. In 2023, fishers near Alaska set up bottom trawlers. Orcas tried to grab the fish. But some orcas got stuck. They were tangled in the fishing gear. Several orcas died.

That's Wild!
FISHING TOGETHER

Orcas and fishers don't always fight over fish. In some cases, the groups work together. Orcas herd other whales near the coast of Australia. They push them toward Twofold Bay. Orcas catch and eat the whales.

For many years, these actions helped humans. The Katungal people lived nearby. They hunted whales for meat. Hunting in deep water was difficult. But killing whales in the shallow bay was easier. Humans thanked the orcas for their help. They tossed the whales' tongues to the orcas.

Whale tongues have proteins that orcas like.

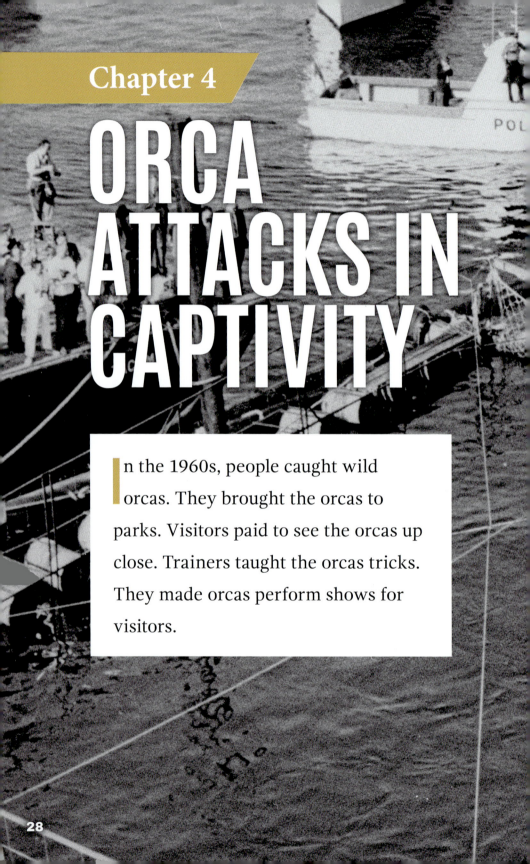

Chapter 4
ORCA ATTACKS IN CAPTIVITY

In the 1960s, people caught wild orcas. They brought the orcas to parks. Visitors paid to see the orcas up close. Trainers taught the orcas tricks. They made orcas perform shows for visitors.

In 1965, Namu became the first captive orca to perform shows. People kept Namu at the Seattle Marine Aquarium.

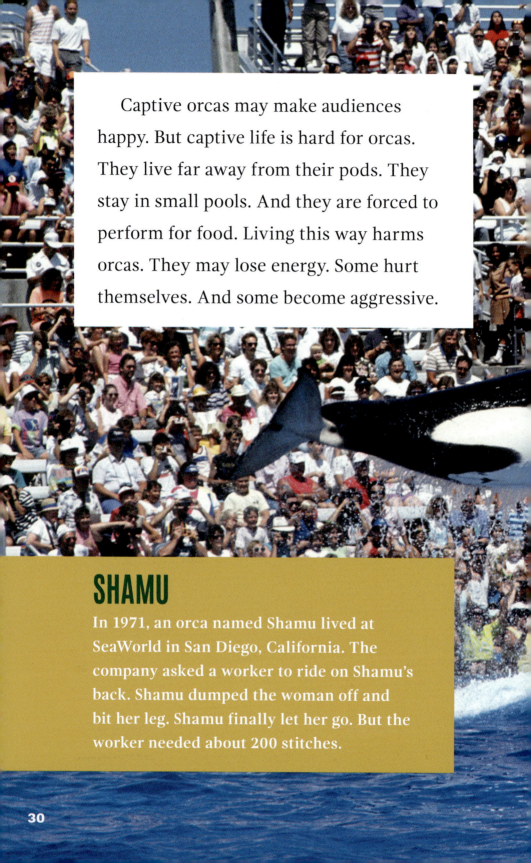

Captive orcas may make audiences happy. But captive life is hard for orcas. They live far away from their pods. They stay in small pools. And they are forced to perform for food. Living this way harms orcas. They may lose energy. Some hurt themselves. And some become aggressive.

SHAMU

In 1971, an orca named Shamu lived at SeaWorld in San Diego, California. The company asked a worker to ride on Shamu's back. Shamu dumped the woman off and bit her leg. Shamu finally let her go. But the worker needed about 200 stitches.

Captive orcas often have to do tricks for people. For example, orcas may flip, jump, and splash on command.

A deadly orca attack happened in 1991. An orca named Tilikum lived at Sealand of the Pacific in Canada. A trainer slipped into the orca pool. Tilikum and two other orcas drowned the trainer. After the attack, Tilikum was sent to SeaWorld in Orlando, Florida. But another disaster happened. A visitor snuck into the orca area at night. Then he drowned in the pool with Tilikum. The man's body showed signs of attack.

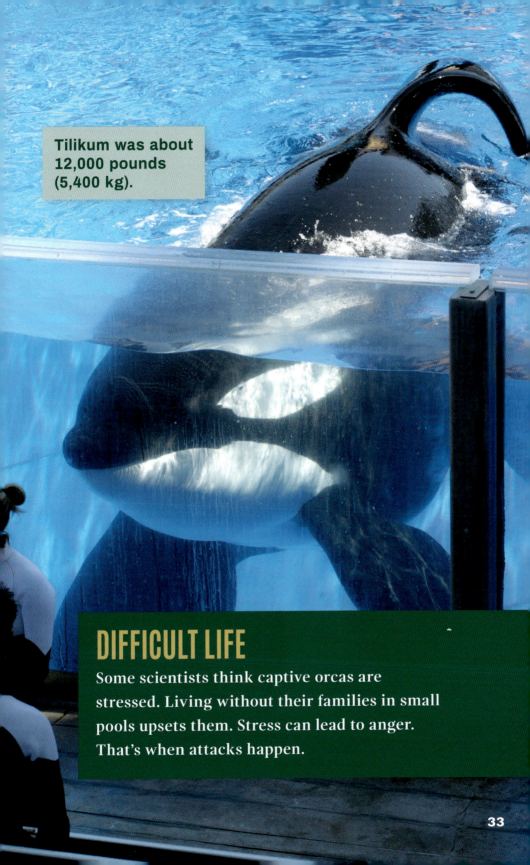

Tilikum was about 12,000 pounds (5,400 kg).

DIFFICULT LIFE

Some scientists think captive orcas are stressed. Living without their families in small pools upsets them. Stress can lead to anger. That's when attacks happen.

Tilikum attacked at SeaWorld one more time. In February 2010, a trainer was playing with Tilikum. But Tilikum dragged the trainer underwater. The orca bit her all over. Other trainers tried to save the woman. But Tilikum did not let go for 45 minutes. The trainer died.

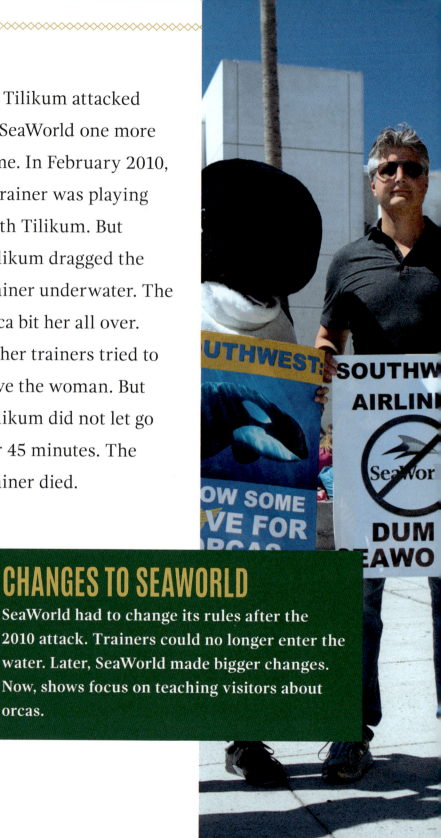

CHANGES TO SEAWORLD
SeaWorld had to change its rules after the 2010 attack. Trainers could no longer enter the water. Later, SeaWorld made bigger changes. Now, shows focus on teaching visitors about orcas.

In 2013, a film about the dangers of captive orcas sparked protests and changes.

Attacks happened in other parts of the world, too. In 2009, an orca attacked a trainer in Tenerife, Spain. The trainer was working with an orca named Keto. He was trying to have Keto do a trick. But Keto kept doing it wrong. He didn't get a reward. The orca was upset. Finally, the orca grabbed the trainer's leg. Keto pulled the man underwater. He drowned.

Many captive orcas have drooping fins. Top fins may curve when orcas spend too much time at the surface of small tanks.

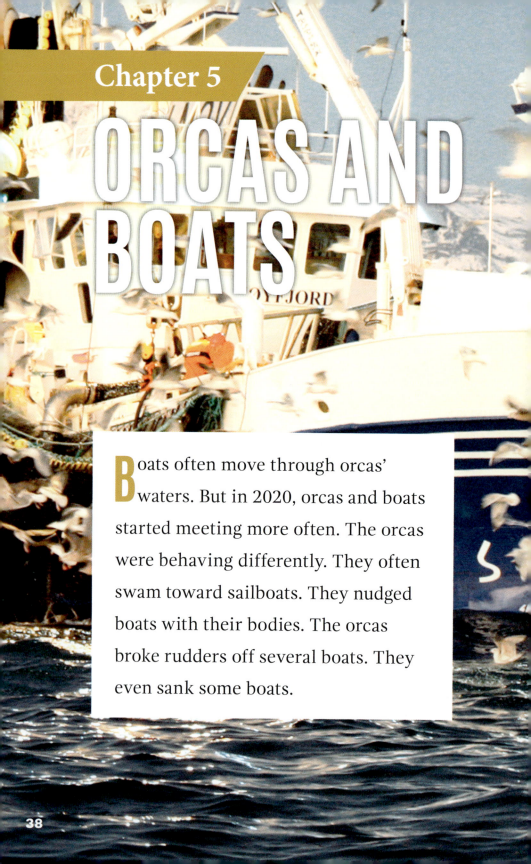

Chapter 5
ORCAS AND BOATS

Boats often move through orcas' waters. But in 2020, orcas and boats started meeting more often. The orcas were behaving differently. They often swam toward sailboats. They nudged boats with their bodies. The orcas broke rudders off several boats. They even sank some boats.

Scientists weren't sure why orcas began hitting boats more often in the early 2020s.

The oldest known orca was named J2, or Granny (above). Scientists guessed that she was 105 years old.

Many of these meetings happened in the Strait of Gibraltar. That area is between Spain and Morocco. One orca was a key part of the events. Her name was White Gladis. White Gladis was an older female in her pod. In 2020, she began approaching boats. Then, she passed the behavior on. She taught younger orcas in her pod.

GRANDMA'S WISDOM
Female orcas may live up to 90 years. As females age, they stay with their pods. They teach their children and grandchildren.

In 2022, a boat race started near Morocco. A group of seven orcas swam toward one boat. The orcas attacked the boat's rudder. They broke the rudder. Then, the orcas swam away. No one was hurt. And luckily, the boat had another rudder. It could still move.

A rudder sits at the back of a boat. It helps steer the ship.

Orcas attack sailboats more often than other boats.

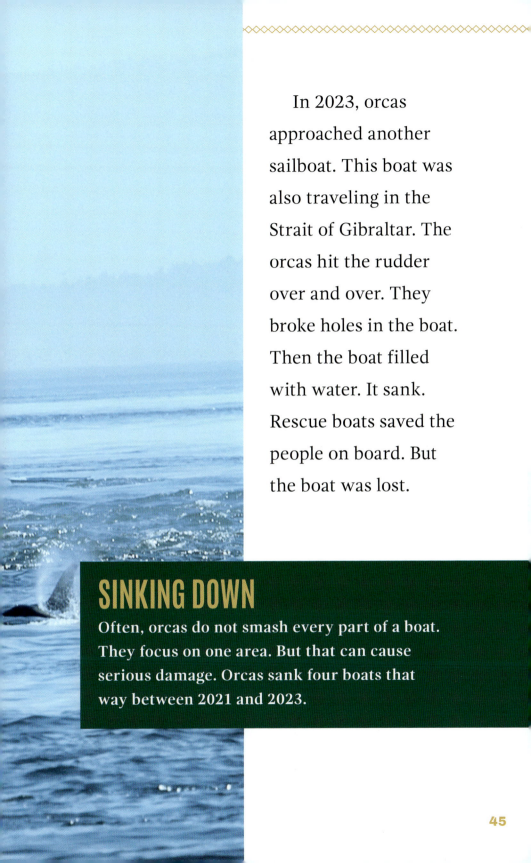

In 2023, orcas approached another sailboat. This boat was also traveling in the Strait of Gibraltar. The orcas hit the rudder over and over. They broke holes in the boat. Then the boat filled with water. It sank. Rescue boats saved the people on board. But the boat was lost.

SINKING DOWN

Often, orcas do not smash every part of a boat. They focus on one area. But that can cause serious damage. Orcas sank four boats that way between 2021 and 2023.

Most of these orca meetings are not attacks. Scientists believe the orcas are just playing. Orcas in the wild play in many ways. Their tails slap the water. They jump out of the water. They may even put salmon on their heads like hats. Touching boats might be a similar action. The orcas see something new to play with.

TUMMY RUBS

Orcas often rub their stomachs on smooth rocks. The motion feels good. So, orcas try similar motions on boats.

Orcas sometimes play with long strands of kelp or ropes from boats.

That's Wild!

HUMANS HELP OUT

In 2002, people spotted a baby orca near Seattle, Washington. The baby needed help. She was alone and sick. So, scientists watched her carefully. They listened to her calls. That helped them learn what type of whale she was. The calls also showed them who her family was.

Next, scientists tested the orca for sickness. They nursed her back to health. When she was well, they returned her to her family. In the 2020s, the orca was still alive. She'd even had babies.

The rescued baby orca was named Springer.

Pollution and overfishing have killed many fish. Orcas cannot find food as easily.

Chapter 6
LIVING TOGETHER

Orcas and humans both need the ocean. But human actions often hurt orcas. Oil spills and trash can harm orcas' prey. Orcas may get sick. They may not have enough to eat. So, cleaning up pollution can help orcas. Companies can also find ways to pollute the water less.

Southern Resident orcas face the biggest danger. They are already endangered. Their main food, salmon, is disappearing. Their habitats are dirty. And boat noise blocks their echolocation. Laws such as the Endangered Species Act helped. The United States passed this law in 1973. It protects endangered species and their habitats.

SAVING THE SOUTHERN

In 2024, only about 75 Southern Resident orcas were left. Scientists were working hard to change that. They hoped to increase salmon and reduce pollution to save these orcas.

People try to clean habitats. Some companies remove trash from oceans.

In 2024, around 56 orcas lived in parks or zoos.

Another law helped orcas and humans over time. In 1972, the United States passed the Marine Mammal Protection Act. This law stopped humans from hurting or killing wild orcas. Some laws also stopped people from catching wild orcas for parks. Those rules meant wild orcas were safer. But it helped humans, too. Over time, fewer orcas lived in theme parks. So, the chances of orcas attacking humans became smaller.

Orcas dislike certain sounds. Some fishers play the sounds to keep orcas away.

New tools can help humans and orcas stay safe. Some sailors track orcas to avoid meetings. Maps show the movements of orca pods. And apps can show where injured whales are. Sailors see this information. Then they can plan their paths. People and orcas can stay safe.

SAFER FISHING

Some new fishing nets are heavier. These weighted nets can keep orcas from getting stuck. That means fewer orcas get hurt. It also means fishers' nets do not break as much. As a result, people lose less money.

MAP

1. North Pacific: Southern Resident orcas feed on salmon.
2. Seattle, Washington: Scientists return a sick baby orca to its pod in 2002.
3. Orlando, Florida: Captive orcas attack humans at SeaWorld in 1991 and 2010.

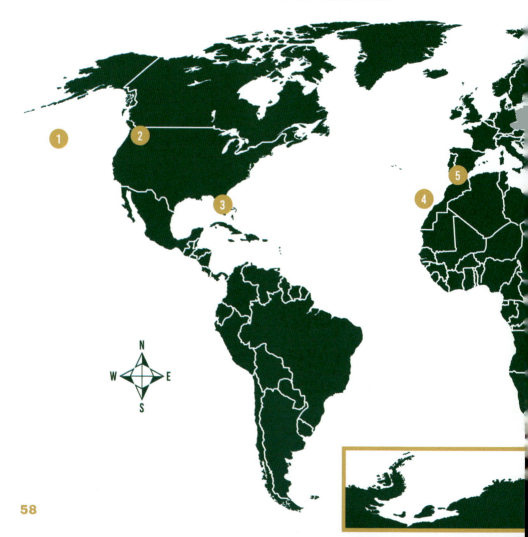

4. Tenerife, Spain: Orcas attack a trainer in 2009.

5. Strait of Gibraltar: Orca pods break rudders and sink boats in the early 2020s.

6. Indian Ocean: Orcas steal fish from longlines.

7. Antarctic: Orcas scare a team of explorers and their dogs in 1911.

8. Twofold Bay, Australia: Orcas herd whales toward shore. Humans give orcas whale tongues in return.

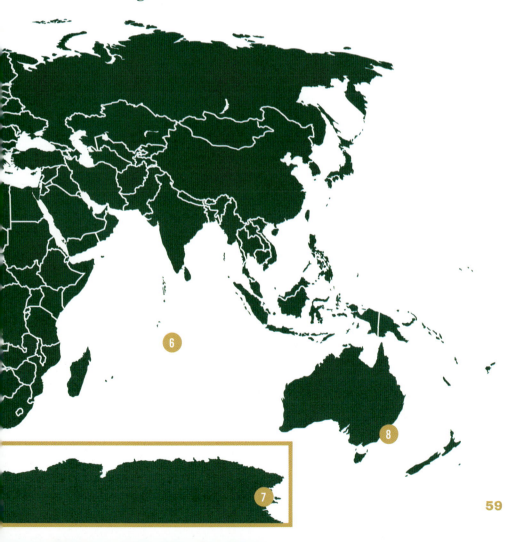

COMPREHENSION QUESTIONS

Write your answers on a separate piece of paper.

1. Write a few sentences describing how orcas hunt.

2. Do you think orcas should be kept in parks? Why or why not?

3. What do Southern Resident orcas mostly eat?

    A. salmon

    B. seals

    C. humans

4. Why did SeaWorld change its orca shows?

    A. The park ran out of wild orcas.

    B. The orcas could not learn any new tricks.

    C. The park did not want more orcas and people to get hurt.

5. What does **stressed** mean in this sentence?

*Some scientists think captive orcas are **stressed**. Living without their families in small pools upsets them. Stress can lead to anger.*

    A. feeling happy
    B. feeling bothered
    C. feeling tired

6. What does **herd** mean in this sentence?

*Orcas **herd** other whales near the coast of Australia. They push them toward Twofold Bay.*

    A. to swim away from something
    B. to make animals move
    C. to turn into something else

Answer key on page 64.

GLOSSARY

aggressive
Strong and quick to attack.

Antarctic
Relating to the very cold and dry region near Antarctica.

captive
Kept in one place by force.

carnivores
Animals that eat meat.

echolocation
The ability to use sound to locate objects.

endangered
In danger of dying out forever.

habitats
The places where animals normally live.

longlines
Long fishing lines with many hooks along them.

mammals
Animals that have hair and produce milk for their young.

pollution
Things that are dirty or unsafe.

prey
Animals that are hunted and eaten by other animals.

rudders
Underwater blades that help steer boats.

TO LEARN MORE

BOOKS

Becker, Trudy. *Orca Pods*. Mendota Heights, MN: Focus Readers, 2025.

Jaycox, Jaclyn. *Orca Cows: Leaders of the Pod*. North Mankato, MN: Pebble, 2022.

Watts, Robyn. *Whales!: The Gentle Giants*. Minneapolis: Lerner Publications, 2024.

ONLINE RESOURCES

Visit **www.apexeditions.com** to find links and resources related to this title.

ABOUT THE AUTHOR

Marie-Therese Miller is an award-winning author of more than 35 nonfiction books for children and teens. Her recent selections include *Sly as a Fox: Are Foxes Clever? Dogs* (An Early Encyclopedia), *Being Thankful with Gabrielle: A Book About Gratitude*, and *Esports Superstars*. Miller earned her PhD in English from St. John's University, where her academic focus was James Thurber's humorous writing. She teaches Children's and YA Literature at Marist College. Miller and her husband have five grown children and a grandson.

INDEX

Alaska, 25
Antarctica, 4, 7
Australia, 26

boats, 14, 19–20, 23, 38, 41–42, 45–46, 52

communication, 9, 13

echolocation, 20, 52

fish, 10, 13–14, 17, 19–20, 23, 25, 26, 46

hunting, 7, 9–10, 13, 17, 19–20, 26

Indian Ocean, 20

Keto, 36

laws, 52, 55

Morocco, 41–42

nets, 25, 57
North Pacific, 19

Orlando, Florida, 32

playing, 46
pods, 9, 13, 20, 30, 33, 41, 48, 57
pollution, 18, 51–52

salmon, 19, 46, 52
San Diego, California, 30
Sealand of the Pacific, 32
Seattle, Washington, 48
SeaWorld, 30, 32, 34
Shamu, 30
Southern Resident orcas, 18–19, 52
Strait of Gibraltar, 41, 45

teeth, 7, 11
Tenerife, Spain, 36
Tilikum, 32, 34
Twofold Bay, Australia, 26

White Gladis, 41

ANSWER KEY:

1. Answers will vary; 2. Answers will vary; 3. A; 4. C; 5. B; 6. B